BARBECUE & SMOKING

LOGBOOK

PITMASTER: ....

....

....

....

PAGE	INDEX

PAGE	INDEX

DATE ....

TITLE
....

MEAT
....

....

NOTES
....

....

WEIGHT
....

WOOD
....

PREPARATION
....

....

MARINADE/RUB
....

....

TIME	SMOKER/MEAT TARGET TEMP.	SMOKER ACTUAL TEMP.	MEAT TEMP.	SMOKER ADJUSTMENT MADE: ADDED COAL, WOOD CHIPS CHUNKS, MOPS, SAUCES, WRAPPED ETC..

TIME	SMOKER/MEAT TARGET TEMP.	SMOKER ACTUAL TEMP.	MEAT TEMP.	SMOKER ADJUSTMENT MADE: ADDED COAL, WOOD CHIPS CHUNKS, MOPS, SAUCES, WRAPPED ETC..

WEATHER
....

COOKING NOTES
....
....
....

RESULTS (AROMA, BARK, FLAVOR, TENDERNESS, MOISTURE, SMOKINESS)
....
....
....
....

RATING   1   2   3   4   5   6   7   8   9   10

ADDITIONAL NOTES (CHANGES, MODIFICATION, THOUGHTS FOR IMPROVING THE NEXT SMOKE)
....
....
....
....
....
....

2

DATE ....

TITLE ....

MEAT ....

....

NOTES ....

....

....

WEIGHT ....

WOOD ....

PREPARATION ....

....

MARINADE/RUB ....

....

TIME	SMOKER/MEAT TARGET TEMP.	SMOKER ACTUAL TEMP.	MEAT TEMP.	SMOKER ADJUSTMENT MADE: ADDED COAL, WOOD CHIPS CHUNKS, MOPS, SAUCES, WRAPPED ETC..

3

TIME	SMOKER/MEAT TARGET TEMP.	SMOKER ACTUAL TEMP.	MEAT TEMP.	SMOKER ADJUSTMENT MADE: ADDED COAL, WOOD CHIPS CHUNKS, MOPS, SAUCES, WRAPPED ETC..

WEATHER

COOKING NOTES

RESULTS (AROMA, BARK, FLAVOR, TENDERNESS, MOISTURE, SMOKINESS)

RATING   1   2   3   4   5   6   7   8   9   10

ADDITIONAL NOTES (CHANGES, MODIFICATION, THOUGHTS FOR IMPROVING THE NEXT SMOKE)

4

DATE ....

TITLE ....

MEAT ....
....

NOTES ....
....

WEIGHT ....

WOOD ....

PREPARATION ....
....

MARINADE/RUB ....
....

TIME	SMOKER/MEAT TARGET TEMP.	SMOKER ACTUAL TEMP.	MEAT TEMP.	SMOKER ADJUSTMENT MADE: ADDED COAL, WOOD CHIPS CHUNKS, MOPS, SAUCES, WRAPPED ETC..

TIME	SMOKER/MEAT TARGET TEMP.	SMOKER ACTUAL TEMP.	MEAT TEMP.	SMOKER ADJUSTMENT MADE: ADDED COAL, WOOD CHIPS CHUNKS, MOPS, SAUCES, WRAPPED ETC..

WEATHER

COOKING NOTES

RESULTS (AROMA, BARK, FLAVOR, TENDERNESS, MOISTURE, SMOKINESS)

RATING   1   2   3   4   5   6   7   8   9   10

ADDITIONAL NOTES (CHANGES, MODIFICATION, THOUGHTS FOR IMPROVING THE NEXT SMOKE)

DATE ....

TITLE
....

MEAT
....
....

NOTES
....
....

WEIGHT
WOOD
....

PREPARATION
....

MARINADE/RUB
....
....

TIME	SMOKER/MEAT TARGET TEMP.	SMOKER ACTUAL TEMP.	MEAT TEMP.	SMOKER ADJUSTMENT MADE: ADDED COAL, WOOD CHIPS CHUNKS, MOPS, SAUCES, WRAPPED ETC..

7

TIME	SMOKER/MEAT TARGET TEMP.	SMOKER ACTUAL TEMP.	MEAT TEMP.	SMOKER ADJUSTMENT MADE: ADDED COAL, WOOD CHIPS CHUNKS, MOPS, SAUCES, WRAPPED ETC..

WEATHER
....

COOKING NOTES
....
....
....

RESULTS (AROMA, BARK, FLAVOR, TENDERNESS, MOISTURE, SMOKINESS)
....
....
....
....

RATING   1   2   3   4   5   6   7   8   9   10

ADDITIONAL NOTES (CHANGES, MODIFICATION, THOUGHTS FOR IMPROVING THE NEXT SMOKE)
....
....
....
....
....

DATE ....

TITLE
....

MEAT
....
....

NOTES
....
....

WEIGHT
....

WOOD
....

PREPARATION
....

MARINADE/RUB
....
....

TIME	SMOKER/MEAT TARGET TEMP.	SMOKER ACTUAL TEMP.	MEAT TEMP.	SMOKER ADJUSTMENT MADE: ADDED COAL, WOOD CHIPS CHUNKS, MOPS, SAUCES, WRAPPED ETC..

TIME	SMOKER/MEAT TARGET TEMP.	SMOKER ACTUAL TEMP.	MEAT TEMP.	SMOKER ADJUSTMENT MADE: ADDED COAL, WOOD CHIPS CHUNKS, MOPS, SAUCES, WRAPPED ETC..

WEATHER
....

COOKING NOTES
....
....
....

RESULTS (AROMA, BARK, FLAVOR, TENDERNESS, MOISTURE, SMOKINESS)
....
....
....
....

RATING 1 2 3 4 5 6 7 8 9 10

ADDITIONAL NOTES (CHANGES, MODIFICATION, THOUGHTS FOR IMPROVING THE NEXT SMOKE)
....
....
....
....
....

DATE ....

TITLE ....

MEAT ....

....

NOTES ....

....

WEIGHT ....

WOOD ....

PREPARATION ....

....

MARINADE/RUB ....

....

TIME	SMOKER/MEAT TARGET TEMP.	SMOKER ACTUAL TEMP.	MEAT TEMP.	SMOKER ADJUSTMENT MADE: ADDED COAL, WOOD CHIPS CHUNKS, MOPS, SAUCES, WRAPPED ETC..

TIME	SMOKER/MEAT TARGET TEMP.	SMOKER ACTUAL TEMP.	MEAT TEMP.	SMOKER ADJUSTMENT MADE: ADDED COAL, WOOD CHIPS CHUNKS, MOPS, SAUCES, WRAPPED ETC..

WEATHER

COOKING NOTES

RESULTS (AROMA, BARK, FLAVOR, TENDERNESS, MOISTURE, SMOKINESS)

RATING   1   2   3   4   5   6   7   8   9   10

ADDITIONAL NOTES (CHANGES, MODIFICATION, THOUGHTS FOR IMPROVING THE NEXT SMOKE)

DATE ....

TITLE
....

MEAT
....

....

NOTES
....

....

WEIGHT
....

WOOD
....

PREPARATION
....

....

MARINADE/RUB
....

....

TIME	SMOKER/MEAT TARGET TEMP.	SMOKER ACTUAL TEMP.	MEAT TEMP.	SMOKER ADJUSTMENT MADE: ADDED COAL, WOOD CHIPS CHUNKS, MOPS, SAUCES, WRAPPED ETC..

13

TIME	SMOKER/MEAT TARGET TEMP.	SMOKER ACTUAL TEMP.	MEAT TEMP.	SMOKER ADJUSTMENT MADE: ADDED COAL, WOOD CHIPS CHUNKS, MOPS, SAUCES, WRAPPED ETC..

WEATHER
....

COOKING NOTES
....
....
....

RESULTS (AROMA, BARK, FLAVOR, TENDERNESS, MOISTURE, SMOKINESS)
....
....
....
....

RATING   1   2   3   4   5   6   7   8   9   10

ADDITIONAL NOTES (CHANGES, MODIFICATION, THOUGHTS FOR IMPROVING THE NEXT SMOKE)
....
....
....
....
....

DATE ....

TITLE
....

MEAT
....

....

NOTES
....

....

WEIGHT
....

WOOD
....

PREPARATION
....

....

MARINADE/RUB
....

....

TIME	SMOKER/MEAT TARGET TEMP.	SMOKER ACTUAL TEMP.	MEAT TEMP.	SMOKER ADJUSTMENT MADE: ADDED COAL, WOOD CHIPS CHUNKS, MOPS, SAUCES, WRAPPED ETC..

TIME	SMOKER/MEAT TARGET TEMP.	SMOKER ACTUAL TEMP.	MEAT TEMP.	SMOKER ADJUSTMENT MADE: ADDED COAL, WOOD CHIPS CHUNKS, MOPS, SAUCES, WRAPPED ETC..

WEATHER

COOKING NOTES

RESULTS (AROMA, BARK, FLAVOR, TENDERNESS, MOISTURE, SMOKINESS)

RATING   1   2   3   4   5   6   7   8   9   10

ADDITIONAL NOTES (CHANGES, MODIFICATION, THOUGHTS FOR IMPROVING THE NEXT SMOKE)

DATE ....

TITLE ....

MEAT ....

....

NOTES ....

....

....

WEIGHT ....

WOOD ....

PREPARATION ....

....

MARINADE/RUB ....

....

TIME	SMOKER/MEAT TARGET TEMP.	SMOKER ACTUAL TEMP.	MEAT TEMP.	SMOKER ADJUSTMENT MADE: ADDED COAL, WOOD CHIPS CHUNKS, MOPS, SAUCES, WRAPPED ETC..

17

TIME	SMOKER/MEAT TARGET TEMP.	SMOKER ACTUAL TEMP.	MEAT TEMP.	SMOKER ADJUSTMENT MADE: ADDED COAL, WOOD CHIPS CHUNKS, MOPS, SAUCES, WRAPPED ETC..

WEATHER
....

COOKING NOTES
....
....
....

RESULTS (AROMA, BARK, FLAVOR, TENDERNESS, MOISTURE, SMOKINESS)
....
....
....
....

RATING   1   2   3   4   5   6   7   8   9   10

ADDITIONAL NOTES (CHANGES, MODIFICATION, THOUGHTS FOR IMPROVING THE NEXT SMOKE)
....
....
....
....
....
....

DATE ....

TITLE
....

MEAT
....

....

NOTES
....

....

....

WEIGHT
....

WOOD
....

PREPARATION
....

....

MARINADE/RUB
....

....

TIME	SMOKER/MEAT TARGET TEMP.	SMOKER ACTUAL TEMP.	MEAT TEMP.	SMOKER ADJUSTMENT MADE: ADDED COAL, WOOD CHIPS CHUNKS, MOPS, SAUCES, WRAPPED ETC..

TIME	SMOKER/MEAT TARGET TEMP.	SMOKER ACTUAL TEMP.	MEAT TEMP.	SMOKER ADJUSTMENT MADE: ADDED COAL, WOOD CHIPS CHUNKS, MOPS, SAUCES, WRAPPED ETC..

WEATHER

COOKING NOTES

RESULTS (AROMA, BARK, FLAVOR, TENDERNESS, MOISTURE, SMOKINESS)

RATING   1   2   3   4   5   6   7   8   9   10

ADDITIONAL NOTES (CHANGES, MODIFICATION, THOUGHTS FOR IMPROVING THE NEXT SMOKE)

DATE ....

TITLE
....

MEAT
....
....

NOTES
....
....
....

WEIGHT
....

WOOD
....

PREPARATION
....
....

MARINADE/RUB
....
....

TIME	SMOKER/MEAT TARGET TEMP.	SMOKER ACTUAL TEMP.	MEAT TEMP.	SMOKER ADJUSTMENT MADE: ADDED COAL, WOOD CHIPS CHUNKS, MOPS, SAUCES, WRAPPED ETC..

21

TIME	SMOKER/MEAT TARGET TEMP.	SMOKER ACTUAL TEMP.	MEAT TEMP.	SMOKER ADJUSTMENT MADE: ADDED COAL, WOOD CHIPS CHUNKS, MOPS, SAUCES, WRAPPED ETC..

WEATHER
....

COOKING NOTES
....
....
....

RESULTS (AROMA, BARK, FLAVOR, TENDERNESS, MOISTURE, SMOKINESS)
....
....
....
....

RATING   1   2   3   4   5   6   7   8   9   10

ADDITIONAL NOTES (CHANGES, MODIFICATION, THOUGHTS FOR IMPROVING THE NEXT SMOKE)
....
....
....
....
....

22

DATE ....

TITLE ....

MEAT ....
....

NOTES ....
....
....

WEIGHT ....

WOOD ....

PREPARATION ....
....

MARINADE/RUB ....
....

TIME	SMOKER/MEAT TARGET TEMP.	SMOKER ACTUAL TEMP.	MEAT TEMP.	SMOKER ADJUSTMENT MADE: ADDED COAL, WOOD CHIPS CHUNKS, MOPS, SAUCES, WRAPPED ETC..

23

TIME	SMOKER/MEAT TARGET TEMP.	SMOKER ACTUAL TEMP.	MEAT TEMP.	SMOKER ADJUSTMENT MADE: ADDED COAL, WOOD CHIPS CHUNKS, MOPS, SAUCES, WRAPPED ETC..

WEATHER
....

COOKING NOTES
....
....
....

RESULTS (AROMA, BARK, FLAVOR, TENDERNESS, MOISTURE, SMOKINESS)
....
....
....
....

RATING   1   2   3   4   5   6   7   8   9   10

ADDITIONAL NOTES (CHANGES, MODIFICATION, THOUGHTS FOR IMPROVING THE NEXT SMOKE)
....
....
....
....
....

DATE ....

TITLE ....

MEAT ....
....

NOTES ....
....
....

WEIGHT ....

WOOD ....

PREPARATION ....
....

MARINADE/RUB ....
....

TIME	SMOKER/MEAT TARGET TEMP.	SMOKER ACTUAL TEMP.	MEAT TEMP.	SMOKER ADJUSTMENT MADE: ADDED COAL, WOOD CHIPS CHUNKS, MOPS, SAUCES, WRAPPED ETC..

TIME	SMOKER/MEAT TARGET TEMP.	SMOKER ACTUAL TEMP.	MEAT TEMP.	SMOKER ADJUSTMENT MADE: ADDED COAL, WOOD CHIPS CHUNKS, MOPS, SAUCES, WRAPPED ETC..

WEATHER
....

COOKING NOTES
....

....

....

RESULTS (AROMA, BARK, FLAVOR, TENDERNESS, MOISTURE, SMOKINESS)
....

....

....

....

RATING   1   2   3   4   5   6   7   8   9   10

ADDITIONAL NOTES (CHANGES, MODIFICATION, THOUGHTS FOR IMPROVING THE NEXT SMOKE)
....

....

....

....

....

DATE ....

TITLE ....

MEAT ....

NOTES ....

....

WEIGHT ....

WOOD ....

PREPARATION ....

MARINADE/RUB ....

....

TIME	SMOKER/MEAT TARGET TEMP.	SMOKER ACTUAL TEMP.	MEAT TEMP.	SMOKER ADJUSTMENT MADE: ADDED COAL, WOOD CHIPS CHUNKS, MOPS, SAUCES, WRAPPED ETC..

TIME	SMOKER/MEAT TARGET TEMP.	SMOKER ACTUAL TEMP.	MEAT TEMP.	SMOKER ADJUSTMENT MADE: ADDED COAL, WOOD CHIPS CHUNKS, MOPS, SAUCES, WRAPPED ETC..

WEATHER
....

COOKING NOTES
....
....
....

RESULTS (AROMA, BARK, FLAVOR, TENDERNESS, MOISTURE, SMOKINESS)
....
....
....
....

RATING   1   2   3   4   5   6   7   8   9   10

ADDITIONAL NOTES (CHANGES, MODIFICATION, THOUGHTS FOR IMPROVING THE NEXT SMOKE)
....
....
....
....
....

DATE ....

TITLE ....

MEAT ....

NOTES ....
....

WEIGHT ....

WOOD ....

PREPARATION ....
....

MARINADE/RUB ....
....

TIME	SMOKER/MEAT TARGET TEMP.	SMOKER ACTUAL TEMP.	MEAT TEMP.	SMOKER ADJUSTMENT MADE: ADDED COAL, WOOD CHIPS CHUNKS, MOPS, SAUCES, WRAPPED ETC..

TIME	SMOKER/MEAT TARGET TEMP.	SMOKER ACTUAL TEMP.	MEAT TEMP.	SMOKER ADJUSTMENT MADE: ADDED COAL, WOOD CHIPS CHUNKS, MOPS, SAUCES, WRAPPED ETC..

WEATHER

COOKING NOTES

RESULTS (AROMA, BARK, FLAVOR, TENDERNESS, MOISTURE, SMOKINESS)

RATING   1   2   3   4   5   6   7   8   9   10

ADDITIONAL NOTES (CHANGES, MODIFICATION, THOUGHTS FOR IMPROVING THE NEXT SMOKE)

DATE ....

TITLE
....

MEAT
....

....

NOTES
....

....

WEIGHT
....

WOOD
....

PREPARATION
....

MARINADE/RUB
....

....

TIME	SMOKER/MEAT TARGET TEMP.	SMOKER ACTUAL TEMP.	MEAT TEMP.	SMOKER ADJUSTMENT MADE: ADDED COAL, WOOD CHIPS CHUNKS, MOPS, SAUCES, WRAPPED ETC..

31

TIME	SMOKER/MEAT TARGET TEMP.	SMOKER ACTUAL TEMP.	MEAT TEMP.	SMOKER ADJUSTMENT MADE: ADDED COAL, WOOD CHIPS CHUNKS, MOPS, SAUCES, WRAPPED ETC..

WEATHER

COOKING NOTES

RESULTS (AROMA, BARK, FLAVOR, TENDERNESS, MOISTURE, SMOKINESS)

RATING   1   2   3   4   5   6   7   8   9   10

ADDITIONAL NOTES (CHANGES, MODIFICATION, THOUGHTS FOR IMPROVING THE NEXT SMOKE)

DATE ....

TITLE ....

MEAT ....
....

NOTES ....
....
....

WEIGHT ....

WOOD ....

PREPARATION ....

MARINADE/RUB ....
....

TIME	SMOKER/MEAT TARGET TEMP.	SMOKER ACTUAL TEMP.	MEAT TEMP.	SMOKER ADJUSTMENT MADE: ADDED COAL, WOOD CHIPS CHUNKS, MOPS, SAUCES, WRAPPED ETC..

TIME	SMOKER/MEAT TARGET TEMP.	SMOKER ACTUAL TEMP.	MEAT TEMP.	SMOKER ADJUSTMENT MADE: ADDED COAL, WOOD CHIPS CHUNKS, MOPS, SAUCES, WRAPPED ETC..

WEATHER
....

COOKING NOTES
....
....
....

RESULTS (AROMA, BARK, FLAVOR, TENDERNESS, MOISTURE, SMOKINESS)
....
....
....
....

RATING   1   2   3   4   5   6   7   8   9   10

ADDITIONAL NOTES (CHANGES, MODIFICATION, THOUGHTS FOR IMPROVING THE NEXT SMOKE)
....
....
....
....
....

DATE ....

TITLE ....

MEAT ....
....

NOTES ....
....
....

WEIGHT ....

WOOD ....

PREPARATION ....
....

MARINADE/RUB ....

....

TIME	SMOKER/MEAT TARGET TEMP.	SMOKER ACTUAL TEMP.	MEAT TEMP.	SMOKER ADJUSTMENT MADE: ADDED COAL, WOOD CHIPS CHUNKS, MOPS, SAUCES, WRAPPED ETC..

TIME	SMOKER/MEAT TARGET TEMP.	SMOKER ACTUAL TEMP.	MEAT TEMP.	SMOKER ADJUSTMENT MADE: ADDED COAL, WOOD CHIPS CHUNKS, MOPS, SAUCES, WRAPPED ETC..

WEATHER

COOKING NOTES

RESULTS (AROMA, BARK, FLAVOR, TENDERNESS, MOISTURE, SMOKINESS)

RATING   1   2   3   4   5   6   7   8   9   10

ADDITIONAL NOTES (CHANGES, MODIFICATION, THOUGHTS FOR IMPROVING THE NEXT SMOKE)

DATE ....

TITLE
....

MEAT
....
....

NOTES
....
....

WEIGHT
....

WOOD
....

PREPARATION
....
....

MARINADE/RUB
....
....

TIME	SMOKER/MEAT TARGET TEMP.	SMOKER ACTUAL TEMP.	MEAT TEMP.	SMOKER ADJUSTMENT MADE: ADDED COAL, WOOD CHIPS CHUNKS, MOPS, SAUCES, WRAPPED ETC..

TIME	SMOKER/MEAT TARGET TEMP.	SMOKER ACTUAL TEMP.	MEAT TEMP.	SMOKER ADJUSTMENT MADE: ADDED COAL, WOOD CHIPS CHUNKS, MOPS, SAUCES, WRAPPED ETC..

WEATHER

COOKING NOTES

RESULTS (AROMA. BARK. FLAVOR. TENDERNESS. MOISTURE. SMOKINESS)

RATING   1   2   3   4   5   6   7   8   9   10

ADDITIONAL NOTES (CHANGES, MODIFICATION, THOUGHTS FOR IMPROVING THE NEXT SMOKE)

DATE ....

TITLE ....

MEAT ....
....

NOTES ....
....

WEIGHT ....

WOOD ....

PREPARATION ....
....

MARINADE/RUB ....
....

TIME	SMOKER/MEAT TARGET TEMP.	SMOKER ACTUAL TEMP.	MEAT TEMP.	SMOKER ADJUSTMENT MADE: ADDED COAL, WOOD CHIPS CHUNKS, MOPS, SAUCES, WRAPPED ETC..

TIME	SMOKER/MEAT TARGET TEMP.	SMOKER ACTUAL TEMP.	MEAT TEMP.	SMOKER ADJUSTMENT MADE: ADDED COAL, WOOD CHIPS CHUNKS, MOPS, SAUCES, WRAPPED ETC..

WEATHER
....

COOKING NOTES
....
....
....

RESULTS (AROMA, BARK, FLAVOR, TENDERNESS, MOISTURE, SMOKINESS)
....
....
....
....

RATING   1   2   3   4   5   6   7   8   9   10

ADDITIONAL NOTES (CHANGES, MODIFICATION, THOUGHTS FOR IMPROVING THE NEXT SMOKE)
....
....
....
....
....

40

DATE ....

TITLE ....

MEAT ....

....

NOTES ....

....

WEIGHT ....

WOOD ....

PREPARATION ....

....

MARINADE/RUB ....

....

TIME	SMOKER/MEAT TARGET TEMP.	SMOKER ACTUAL TEMP.	MEAT TEMP.	SMOKER ADJUSTMENT MADE: ADDED COAL, WOOD CHIPS CHUNKS, MOPS, SAUCES, WRAPPED ETC..

41

TIME	SMOKER/MEAT TARGET TEMP.	SMOKER ACTUAL TEMP.	MEAT TEMP.	SMOKER ADJUSTMENT MADE: ADDED COAL, WOOD CHIPS CHUNKS, MOPS, SAUCES, WRAPPED ETC..

WEATHER
....

COOKING NOTES
....
....
....

RESULTS (AROMA, BARK, FLAVOR, TENDERNESS, MOISTURE, SMOKINESS)
....
....
....
....

RATING   1   2   3   4   5   6   7   8   9   10

ADDITIONAL NOTES (CHANGES, MODIFICATION, THOUGHTS FOR IMPROVING THE NEXT SMOKE)
....
....
....
....
....

DATE ....

TITLE
....

MEAT
....

NOTES
....

....

WEIGHT
....

WOOD
....

PREPARATION
....

MARINADE/RUB
....

....

TIME	SMOKER/MEAT TARGET TEMP.	SMOKER ACTUAL TEMP.	MEAT TEMP.	SMOKER ADJUSTMENT MADE: ADDED COAL, WOOD CHIPS CHUNKS, MOPS, SAUCES, WRAPPED ETC..

TIME	SMOKER/MEAT TARGET TEMP.	SMOKER ACTUAL TEMP.	MEAT TEMP.	SMOKER ADJUSTMENT MADE: ADDED COAL, WOOD CHIPS CHUNKS, MOPS, SAUCES, WRAPPED ETC..

WEATHER
....

COOKING NOTES
....
....
....

RESULTS (AROMA, BARK, FLAVOR, TENDERNESS, MOISTURE, SMOKINESS)
....
....
....
....

RATING   1   2   3   4   5   6   7   8   9   10

ADDITIONAL NOTES (CHANGES, MODIFICATION, THOUGHTS FOR IMPROVING THE NEXT SMOKE)
....
....
....
....
....

DATE ....

TITLE
....

MEAT
....

NOTES
....

....

WEIGHT
....

WOOD
....

PREPARATION
....

MARINADE/RUB
....

....

TIME	SMOKER/MEAT TARGET TEMP.	SMOKER ACTUAL TEMP.	MEAT TEMP.	SMOKER ADJUSTMENT MADE: ADDED COAL, WOOD CHIPS CHUNKS, MOPS, SAUCES, WRAPPED ETC..

45

TIME	SMOKER/MEAT TARGET TEMP.	SMOKER ACTUAL TEMP.	MEAT TEMP.	SMOKER ADJUSTMENT MADE: ADDED COAL, WOOD CHIPS CHUNKS, MOPS, SAUCES, WRAPPED ETC..

WEATHER
....

COOKING NOTES
....
....
....

RESULTS (AROMA, BARK, FLAVOR, TENDERNESS, MOISTURE, SMOKINESS)
....
....
....
....

RATING   1   2   3   4   5   6   7   8   9   10

ADDITIONAL NOTES (CHANGES, MODIFICATION, THOUGHTS FOR IMPROVING THE NEXT SMOKE)
....
....
....
....
....

DATE ....

TITLE ....

MEAT ....

....

NOTES ....

....

WEIGHT ....

WOOD ....

PREPARATION ....

....

MARINADE/RUB ....

....

TIME	SMOKER/MEAT TARGET TEMP.	SMOKER ACTUAL TEMP.	MEAT TEMP.	SMOKER ADJUSTMENT MADE: ADDED COAL, WOOD CHIPS CHUNKS, MOPS, SAUCES, WRAPPED ETC..

TIME	SMOKER/MEAT TARGET TEMP.	SMOKER ACTUAL TEMP.	MEAT TEMP.	SMOKER ADJUSTMENT MADE: ADDED COAL, WOOD CHIPS CHUNKS, MOPS, SAUCES, WRAPPED ETC..

WEATHER

COOKING NOTES

RESULTS (AROMA, BARK, FLAVOR, TENDERNESS, MOISTURE, SMOKINESS)

RATING   1   2   3   4   5   6   7   8   9   10

ADDITIONAL NOTES (CHANGES, MODIFICATION, THOUGHTS FOR IMPROVING THE NEXT SMOKE)

DATE ....

TITLE
....

MEAT
....

....

NOTES
....

....

WEIGHT
....

WOOD
....

PREPARATION
....

....

MARINADE/RUB
....

....

TIME	SMOKER/MEAT TARGET TEMP.	SMOKER ACTUAL TEMP.	MEAT TEMP.	SMOKER ADJUSTMENT MADE: ADDED COAL, WOOD CHIPS CHUNKS, MOPS, SAUCES, WRAPPED ETC..

TIME	SMOKER/MEAT TARGET TEMP.	SMOKER ACTUAL TEMP.	MEAT TEMP.	SMOKER ADJUSTMENT MADE: ADDED COAL, WOOD CHIPS CHUNKS, MOPS, SAUCES, WRAPPED ETC..

WEATHER
....

COOKING NOTES
....

....

....

RESULTS (AROMA, BARK, FLAVOR, TENDERNESS, MOISTURE, SMOKINESS)
....

....

....

....

RATING   1   2   3   4   5   6   7   8   9   10

ADDITIONAL NOTES (CHANGES, MODIFICATION, THOUGHTS FOR IMPROVING THE NEXT SMOKE)
....

....

....

....

....

DATE ....

TITLE ....

MEAT ....

....

NOTES ....

....

WEIGHT ....

WOOD ....

PREPARATION ....

....

MARINADE/RUB ....

....

TIME	SMOKER/MEAT TARGET TEMP.	SMOKER ACTUAL TEMP.	MEAT TEMP.	SMOKER ADJUSTMENT MADE: ADDED COAL, WOOD CHIPS CHUNKS, MOPS, SAUCES, WRAPPED ETC..

51

TIME	SMOKER/MEAT TARGET TEMP.	SMOKER ACTUAL TEMP.	MEAT TEMP.	SMOKER ADJUSTMENT MADE: ADDED COAL, WOOD CHIPS CHUNKS, MOPS, SAUCES, WRAPPED ETC..

WEATHER
....

COOKING NOTES
....
....
....

RESULTS (AROMA, BARK, FLAVOR, TENDERNESS, MOISTURE, SMOKINESS)
....
....
....
....

RATING   1   2   3   4   5   6   7   8   9   10

ADDITIONAL NOTES (CHANGES, MODIFICATION, THOUGHTS FOR IMPROVING THE NEXT SMOKE)
....
....
....
....
....

DATE ....

TITLE
....

MEAT
....

....

NOTES
....

....

WEIGHT
....

WOOD
....

PREPARATION
....

....

MARINADE/RUB
....

....

TIME	SMOKER/MEAT TARGET TEMP.	SMOKER ACTUAL TEMP.	MEAT TEMP.	SMOKER ADJUSTMENT MADE: ADDED COAL, WOOD CHIPS CHUNKS, MOPS, SAUCES, WRAPPED ETC..

TIME	SMOKER/MEAT TARGET TEMP.	SMOKER ACTUAL TEMP.	MEAT TEMP.	SMOKER ADJUSTMENT MADE: ADDED COAL, WOOD CHIPS CHUNKS, MOPS, SAUCES, WRAPPED ETC..

WEATHER
....

COOKING NOTES
....
....
....

RESULTS (AROMA, BARK, FLAVOR, TENDERNESS, MOISTURE, SMOKINESS)
....
....
....
....

RATING   1   2   3   4   5   6   7   8   9   10

ADDITIONAL NOTES (CHANGES, MODIFICATION, THOUGHTS FOR IMPROVING THE NEXT SMOKE)
....
....
....
....
....

DATE ....

TITLE ....

MEAT ....
....

NOTES ....
....

WEIGHT ....

WOOD ....

PREPARATION ....
....

MARINADE/RUB ....
....

TIME	SMOKER/MEAT TARGET TEMP.	SMOKER ACTUAL TEMP.	MEAT TEMP.	SMOKER ADJUSTMENT MADE: ADDED COAL, WOOD CHIPS CHUNKS, MOPS, SAUCES, WRAPPED ETC..

TIME	SMOKER/MEAT TARGET TEMP.	SMOKER ACTUAL TEMP.	MEAT TEMP.	SMOKER ADJUSTMENT MADE: ADDED COAL, WOOD CHIPS CHUNKS, MOPS, SAUCES, WRAPPED ETC..

WEATHER
....

COOKING NOTES
....
....
....

RESULTS (AROMA, BARK, FLAVOR, TENDERNESS, MOISTURE, SMOKINESS)
....
....
....
....

RATING   1   2   3   4   5   6   7   8   9   10

ADDITIONAL NOTES (CHANGES, MODIFICATION, THOUGHTS FOR IMPROVING THE NEXT SMOKE)
....
....
....
....
....

DATE ....

TITLE ....

MEAT ....

NOTES ....
....

WEIGHT ....

WOOD ....

PREPARATION ....

MARINADE/RUB ....
....

TIME	SMOKER/MEAT TARGET TEMP.	SMOKER ACTUAL TEMP.	MEAT TEMP.	SMOKER ADJUSTMENT MADE: ADDED COAL, WOOD CHIPS CHUNKS, MOPS, SAUCES, WRAPPED ETC..

TIME	SMOKER/MEAT TARGET TEMP.	SMOKER ACTUAL TEMP.	MEAT TEMP.	SMOKER ADJUSTMENT MADE: ADDED COAL, WOOD CHIPS CHUNKS, MOPS, SAUCES, WRAPPED ETC..

WEATHER
....

COOKING NOTES
....
....
....

RESULTS (AROMA, BARK, FLAVOR, TENDERNESS, MOISTURE, SMOKINESS)
....
....
....
....

RATING   1   2   3   4   5   6   7   8   9   10

ADDITIONAL NOTES (CHANGES, MODIFICATION, THOUGHTS FOR IMPROVING THE NEXT SMOKE)
....
....
....
....
....

DATE ....

TITLE ....

MEAT ....

....

NOTES ....

....

WEIGHT ....

WOOD ....

PREPARATION ....

....

MARINADE/RUB ....

....

TIME	SMOKER/MEAT TARGET TEMP.	SMOKER ACTUAL TEMP.	MEAT TEMP.	SMOKER ADJUSTMENT MADE: ADDED COAL, WOOD CHIPS CHUNKS, MOPS, SAUCES, WRAPPED ETC..

TIME	SMOKER/MEAT TARGET TEMP.	SMOKER ACTUAL TEMP.	MEAT TEMP.	SMOKER ADJUSTMENT MADE: ADDED COAL, WOOD CHIPS CHUNKS, MOPS, SAUCES, WRAPPED ETC..

WEATHER

COOKING NOTES

RESULTS (AROMA, BARK, FLAVOR, TENDERNESS, MOISTURE, SMOKINESS)

RATING   1   2   3   4   5   6   7   8   9   10

ADDITIONAL NOTES (CHANGES, MODIFICATION, THOUGHTS FOR IMPROVING THE NEXT SMOKE)

DATE ....

TITLE ....

MEAT ....

NOTES ....
....
....

WEIGHT ....

WOOD ....

PREPARATION ....
....

MARINADE/RUB ....
....

TIME	SMOKER/MEAT TARGET TEMP.	SMOKER ACTUAL TEMP.	MEAT TEMP.	SMOKER ADJUSTMENT MADE: ADDED COAL, WOOD CHIPS CHUNKS, MOPS, SAUCES, WRAPPED ETC..

TIME	SMOKER/MEAT TARGET TEMP.	SMOKER ACTUAL TEMP.	MEAT TEMP.	SMOKER ADJUSTMENT MADE: ADDED COAL, WOOD CHIPS CHUNKS, MOPS, SAUCES, WRAPPED ETC..

WEATHER

COOKING NOTES

RESULTS (AROMA. BARK. FLAVOR. TENDERNESS. MOISTURE. SMOKINESS)

RATING   1   2   3   4   5   6   7   8   9   10

ADDITIONAL NOTES (CHANGES. MODIFICATION. THOUGHTS FOR IMPROVING THE NEXT SMOKE)

DATE ....

TITLE ....

MEAT ....

....

NOTES ....

....

WEIGHT ....

WOOD ....

PREPARATION ....

....

MARINADE/RUB ....

....

TIME	SMOKER/MEAT TARGET TEMP.	SMOKER ACTUAL TEMP.	MEAT TEMP.	SMOKER ADJUSTMENT MADE: ADDED COAL, WOOD CHIPS CHUNKS, MOPS, SAUCES, WRAPPED ETC..

TIME	SMOKER/MEAT TARGET TEMP.	SMOKER ACTUAL TEMP.	MEAT TEMP.	SMOKER ADJUSTMENT MADE: ADDED COAL, WOOD CHIPS CHUNKS, MOPS, SAUCES, WRAPPED ETC..

WEATHER
....

COOKING NOTES
....
....
....

RESULTS (AROMA, BARK, FLAVOR, TENDERNESS, MOISTURE, SMOKINESS)
....
....
....
....

RATING   1   2   3   4   5   6   7   8   9   10

ADDITIONAL NOTES (CHANGES, MODIFICATION, THOUGHTS FOR IMPROVING THE NEXT SMOKE)
....
....
....
....
....

DATE ....

TITLE ....

MEAT ....

NOTES ....
....

WEIGHT ....

WOOD ....

PREPARATION ....
....

MARINADE/RUB ....
....

TIME	SMOKER/MEAT TARGET TEMP.	SMOKER ACTUAL TEMP.	MEAT TEMP.	SMOKER ADJUSTMENT MADE: ADDED COAL, WOOD CHIPS CHUNKS, MOPS, SAUCES, WRAPPED ETC..

TIME	SMOKER/MEAT TARGET TEMP.	SMOKER ACTUAL TEMP.	MEAT TEMP.	SMOKER ADJUSTMENT MADE: ADDED COAL, WOOD CHIPS CHUNKS, MOPS, SAUCES, WRAPPED ETC..

WEATHER
....

COOKING NOTES
....
....
....

RESULTS (AROMA, BARK, FLAVOR, TENDERNESS, MOISTURE, SMOKINESS)
....
....
....
....

RATING   1   2   3   4   5   6   7   8   9   10

ADDITIONAL NOTES (CHANGES, MODIFICATION, THOUGHTS FOR IMPROVING THE NEXT SMOKE)
....
....
....
....
....

66

DATE ....

TITLE ....

MEAT ....
....

NOTES ....
....

WEIGHT ....

WOOD ....

PREPARATION ....
....

MARINADE/RUB ....
....

TIME	SMOKER/MEAT TARGET TEMP.	SMOKER ACTUAL TEMP.	MEAT TEMP.	SMOKER ADJUSTMENT MADE: ADDED COAL, WOOD CHIPS CHUNKS, MOPS, SAUCES, WRAPPED ETC..

67

TIME	SMOKER/MEAT TARGET TEMP.	SMOKER ACTUAL TEMP.	MEAT TEMP.	SMOKER ADJUSTMENT MADE: ADDED COAL, WOOD CHIPS CHUNKS, MOPS, SAUCES, WRAPPED ETC..

WEATHER

COOKING NOTES

RESULTS (AROMA, BARK, FLAVOR, TENDERNESS, MOISTURE, SMOKINESS)

RATING   1   2   3   4   5   6   7   8   9   10

ADDITIONAL NOTES (CHANGES, MODIFICATION, THOUGHTS FOR IMPROVING THE NEXT SMOKE)

DATE ....

TITLE

MEAT

NOTES

WEIGHT

WOOD

PREPARATION

MARINADE/RUB

TIME	SMOKER/MEAT TARGET TEMP.	SMOKER ACTUAL TEMP.	MEAT TEMP.	SMOKER ADJUSTMENT MADE: ADDED COAL, WOOD CHIPS CHUNKS, MOPS, SAUCES, WRAPPED ETC..

TIME	SMOKER/MEAT TARGET TEMP.	SMOKER ACTUAL TEMP.	MEAT TEMP.	SMOKER ADJUSTMENT MADE: ADDED COAL, WOOD CHIPS CHUNKS, MOPS, SAUCES, WRAPPED ETC..

WEATHER
....

COOKING NOTES
....
....
....

RESULTS (AROMA, BARK, FLAVOR, TENDERNESS, MOISTURE, SMOKINESS)
....
....
....
....

RATING   1   2   3   4   5   6   7   8   9   10

ADDITIONAL NOTES (CHANGES, MODIFICATION, THOUGHTS FOR IMPROVING THE NEXT SMOKE)
....
....
....
....
....

DATE ....

TITLE ....

MEAT ....
....

NOTES ....
....

WEIGHT ....

WOOD ....

PREPARATION ....
....

MARINADE/RUB ....
....

TIME	SMOKER/MEAT TARGET TEMP.	SMOKER ACTUAL TEMP.	MEAT TEMP.	SMOKER ADJUSTMENT MADE: ADDED COAL, WOOD CHIPS CHUNKS, MOPS, SAUCES, WRAPPED ETC..

TIME	SMOKER/MEAT TARGET TEMP.	SMOKER ACTUAL TEMP.	MEAT TEMP.	SMOKER ADJUSTMENT MADE: ADDED COAL, WOOD CHIPS CHUNKS, MOPS, SAUCES, WRAPPED ETC..

WEATHER
....

COOKING NOTES
....
....
....

RESULTS (AROMA, BARK, FLAVOR, TENDERNESS, MOISTURE, SMOKINESS)
....
....
....
....

RATING   1   2   3   4   5   6   7   8   9   10

ADDITIONAL NOTES (CHANGES, MODIFICATION, THOUGHTS FOR IMPROVING THE NEXT SMOKE)
....
....
....
....
....

DATE ....

TITLE ....

MEAT ....

....

NOTES ....

....

WEIGHT ....

WOOD ....

PREPARATION ....

MARINADE/RUB ....

....

TIME	SMOKER/MEAT TARGET TEMP.	SMOKER ACTUAL TEMP.	MEAT TEMP.	SMOKER ADJUSTMENT MADE: ADDED COAL, WOOD CHIPS CHUNKS, MOPS, SAUCES, WRAPPED ETC..

TIME	SMOKER/MEAT TARGET TEMP.	SMOKER ACTUAL TEMP.	MEAT TEMP.	SMOKER ADJUSTMENT MADE: ADDED COAL, WOOD CHIPS CHUNKS, MOPS, SAUCES, WRAPPED ETC..

WEATHER
....

COOKING NOTES
....
....
....

RESULTS (AROMA, BARK, FLAVOR, TENDERNESS, MOISTURE, SMOKINESS)
....
....
....
....

RATING   1   2   3   4   5   6   7   8   9   10

ADDITIONAL NOTES (CHANGES, MODIFICATION, THOUGHTS FOR IMPROVING THE NEXT SMOKE)
....
....
....
....
....

DATE ....

TITLE
....

MEAT
....
....

NOTES
....
....

WEIGHT
....

WOOD
....

PREPARATION
....
....

MARINADE/RUB
....
....

TIME	SMOKER/MEAT TARGET TEMP.	SMOKER ACTUAL TEMP.	MEAT TEMP.	SMOKER ADJUSTMENT MADE: ADDED COAL, WOOD CHIPS CHUNKS, MOPS, SAUCES, WRAPPED ETC..

TIME	SMOKER/MEAT TARGET TEMP.	SMOKER ACTUAL TEMP.	MEAT TEMP.	SMOKER ADJUSTMENT MADE: ADDED COAL, WOOD CHIPS CHUNKS, MOPS, SAUCES, WRAPPED ETC..

WEATHER
....

COOKING NOTES
....
....
....

RESULTS (AROMA, BARK, FLAVOR, TENDERNESS, MOISTURE, SMOKINESS)
....
....
....
....

RATING   1   2   3   4   5   6   7   8   9   10

ADDITIONAL NOTES (CHANGES, MODIFICATION, THOUGHTS FOR IMPROVING THE NEXT SMOKE)
....
....
....
....
....

DATE ....

TITLE
....

MEAT
....

NOTES
....
....

WEIGHT
....

WOOD

PREPARATION
....
....

MARINADE/RUB
....

....

TIME	SMOKER/MEAT TARGET TEMP.	SMOKER ACTUAL TEMP.	MEAT TEMP.	SMOKER ADJUSTMENT MADE: ADDED COAL, WOOD CHIPS CHUNKS, MOPS, SAUCES, WRAPPED ETC..

TIME	SMOKER/MEAT TARGET TEMP.	SMOKER ACTUAL TEMP.	MEAT TEMP.	SMOKER ADJUSTMENT MADE: ADDED COAL, WOOD CHIPS CHUNKS, MOPS, SAUCES, WRAPPED ETC..

WEATHER
....

COOKING NOTES
....
....
....

RESULTS (AROMA, BARK, FLAVOR, TENDERNESS, MOISTURE, SMOKINESS)
....
....
....
....

RATING   1   2   3   4   5   6   7   8   9   10

ADDITIONAL NOTES (CHANGES, MODIFICATION, THOUGHTS FOR IMPROVING THE NEXT SMOKE)
....
....
....
....
....

DATE ....

TITLE
....

MEAT
....

....

NOTES
....

....

WEIGHT
....

WOOD
....

PREPARATION
....

....

MARINADE/RUB
....

....

TIME	SMOKER/MEAT TARGET TEMP.	SMOKER ACTUAL TEMP.	MEAT TEMP.	SMOKER ADJUSTMENT MADE: ADDED COAL, WOOD CHIPS CHUNKS, MOPS, SAUCES, WRAPPED ETC..

79

TIME	SMOKER/MEAT TARGET TEMP.	SMOKER ACTUAL TEMP.	MEAT TEMP.	SMOKER ADJUSTMENT MADE: ADDED COAL, WOOD CHIPS CHUNKS, MOPS, SAUCES, WRAPPED ETC..

WEATHER
....

COOKING NOTES
....
....
....

RESULTS (AROMA, BARK, FLAVOR, TENDERNESS, MOISTURE, SMOKINESS)
....
....
....
....

RATING   1   2   3   4   5   6   7   8   9   10

ADDITIONAL NOTES (CHANGES, MODIFICATION, THOUGHTS FOR IMPROVING THE NEXT SMOKE)
....
....
....
....
....

DATE ....

TITLE
....

MEAT
....
....

NOTES
....
....
....

WEIGHT
....

WOOD
....

PREPARATION
....
....

MARINADE/RUB
....
....

TIME	SMOKER/MEAT TARGET TEMP.	SMOKER ACTUAL TEMP.	MEAT TEMP.	SMOKER ADJUSTMENT MADE: ADDED COAL, WOOD CHIPS CHUNKS, MOPS, SAUCES, WRAPPED ETC..

81

TIME	SMOKER/MEAT TARGET TEMP.	SMOKER ACTUAL TEMP.	MEAT TEMP.	SMOKER ADJUSTMENT MADE: ADDED COAL, WOOD CHIPS CHUNKS, MOPS, SAUCES, WRAPPED ETC..

WEATHER ....

COOKING NOTES ....

....

....

RESULTS (AROMA, BARK, FLAVOR, TENDERNESS, MOISTURE, SMOKINESS)
....

....

....

....

RATING 1 2 3 4 5 6 7 8 9 10

ADDITIONAL NOTES (CHANGES, MODIFICATION, THOUGHTS FOR IMPROVING THE NEXT SMOKE)
....

....

....

....

....

DATE ....

TITLE ....

MEAT ....
....

NOTES ....
....
....

WEIGHT ....

WOOD ....

PREPARATION ....
....

MARINADE/RUB ....
....

TIME	SMOKER/MEAT TARGET TEMP.	SMOKER ACTUAL TEMP.	MEAT TEMP.	SMOKER ADJUSTMENT MADE: ADDED COAL, WOOD CHIPS CHUNKS, MOPS, SAUCES, WRAPPED ETC..

83

TIME	SMOKER/MEAT TARGET TEMP.	SMOKER ACTUAL TEMP.	MEAT TEMP.	SMOKER ADJUSTMENT MADE: ADDED COAL, WOOD CHIPS CHUNKS, MOPS, SAUCES, WRAPPED ETC..

WEATHER
....

COOKING NOTES
....
....
....

RESULTS (AROMA, BARK, FLAVOR, TENDERNESS, MOISTURE, SMOKINESS)
....
....
....
....

RATING　　1　　2　　3　　4　　5　　6　　7　　8　　9　　10

ADDITIONAL NOTES (CHANGES, MODIFICATION, THOUGHTS FOR IMPROVING THE NEXT SMOKE)
....
....
....
....
....

DATE ....

TITLE
....

MEAT
....

NOTES
....
....

WEIGHT
....

WOOD
....

PREPARATION
....

MARINADE/RUB
....

TIME	SMOKER/MEAT TARGET TEMP.	SMOKER ACTUAL TEMP.	MEAT TEMP.	SMOKER ADJUSTMENT MADE: ADDED COAL, WOOD CHIPS CHUNKS, MOPS, SAUCES, WRAPPED ETC..

TIME	SMOKER/MEAT TARGET TEMP.	SMOKER ACTUAL TEMP.	MEAT TEMP.	SMOKER ADJUSTMENT MADE: ADDED COAL, WOOD CHIPS CHUNKS, MOPS, SAUCES, WRAPPED ETC..

WEATHER
....

COOKING NOTES
....
....
....

RESULTS (AROMA, BARK, FLAVOR, TENDERNESS, MOISTURE, SMOKINESS)
....
....
....
....

RATING   1   2   3   4   5   6   7   8   9   10

ADDITIONAL NOTES (CHANGES, MODIFICATION, THOUGHTS FOR IMPROVING THE NEXT SMOKE)
....
....
....
....
....

DATE ....

TITLE ....

MEAT ....

....

NOTES ....

....

WEIGHT ....

WOOD ....

PREPARATION ....

....

MARINADE/RUB ....

....

TIME	SMOKER/MEAT TARGET TEMP.	SMOKER ACTUAL TEMP.	MEAT TEMP.	SMOKER ADJUSTMENT MADE: ADDED COAL, WOOD CHIPS CHUNKS, MOPS, SAUCES, WRAPPED ETC..

TIME	SMOKER/MEAT TARGET TEMP.	SMOKER ACTUAL TEMP.	MEAT TEMP.	SMOKER ADJUSTMENT MADE: ADDED COAL, WOOD CHIPS CHUNKS, MOPS, SAUCES, WRAPPED ETC..

WEATHER
....

COOKING NOTES
....
....
....

RESULTS (AROMA, BARK, FLAVOR, TENDERNESS, MOISTURE, SMOKINESS)
....
....
....
....

RATING   1   2   3   4   5   6   7   8   9   10

ADDITIONAL NOTES (CHANGES, MODIFICATION, THOUGHTS FOR IMPROVING THE NEXT SMOKE)
....
....
....
....
....

DATE ....

TITLE ....

MEAT ....

....

NOTES ....

....

WEIGHT ....

WOOD ....

PREPARATION ....

....

MARINADE/RUB ....

....

TIME	SMOKER/MEAT TARGET TEMP.	SMOKER ACTUAL TEMP.	MEAT TEMP.	SMOKER ADJUSTMENT MADE: ADDED COAL, WOOD CHIPS CHUNKS, MOPS, SAUCES, WRAPPED ETC..

TIME	SMOKER/MEAT TARGET TEMP.	SMOKER ACTUAL TEMP.	MEAT TEMP.	SMOKER ADJUSTMENT MADE: ADDED COAL, WOOD CHIPS CHUNKS, MOPS, SAUCES, WRAPPED ETC..

WEATHER

COOKING NOTES

RESULTS (AROMA, BARK, FLAVOR, TENDERNESS, MOISTURE, SMOKINESS)

RATING   1   2   3   4   5   6   7   8   9   10

ADDITIONAL NOTES (CHANGES, MODIFICATION, THOUGHTS FOR IMPROVING THE NEXT SMOKE)

90

DATE ....

TITLE ....

MEAT ....

....

NOTES ....

....

WEIGHT ....

WOOD ....

PREPARATION ....

MARINADE/RUB ....

....

TIME	SMOKER/MEAT TARGET TEMP.	SMOKER ACTUAL TEMP.	MEAT TEMP.	SMOKER ADJUSTMENT MADE: ADDED COAL, WOOD CHIPS CHUNKS, MOPS, SAUCES, WRAPPED ETC..

TIME	SMOKER/MEAT TARGET TEMP.	SMOKER ACTUAL TEMP.	MEAT TEMP.	SMOKER ADJUSTMENT MADE: ADDED COAL, WOOD CHIPS CHUNKS, MOPS, SAUCES, WRAPPED ETC..

WEATHER

COOKING NOTES

RESULTS (AROMA, BARK, FLAVOR, TENDERNESS, MOISTURE, SMOKINESS)

RATING   1   2   3   4   5   6   7   8   9   10

ADDITIONAL NOTES (CHANGES, MODIFICATION, THOUGHTS FOR IMPROVING THE NEXT SMOKE)

DATE ....

TITLE ....

MEAT ....

NOTES ....

....

WEIGHT ....

WOOD ....

PREPARATION ....

....

MARINADE/RUB ....

....

TIME	SMOKER/MEAT TARGET TEMP.	SMOKER ACTUAL TEMP.	MEAT TEMP.	SMOKER ADJUSTMENT MADE: ADDED COAL, WOOD CHIPS CHUNKS, MOPS, SAUCES, WRAPPED ETC..

TIME	SMOKER/MEAT TARGET TEMP.	SMOKER ACTUAL TEMP.	MEAT TEMP.	SMOKER ADJUSTMENT MADE: ADDED COAL, WOOD CHIPS CHUNKS, MOPS, SAUCES, WRAPPED ETC..

WEATHER
....

COOKING NOTES
....
....
....

RESULTS (AROMA, BARK, FLAVOR, TENDERNESS, MOISTURE, SMOKINESS)
....
....
....
....

RATING   1   2   3   4   5   6   7   8   9   10

ADDITIONAL NOTES (CHANGES, MODIFICATION, THOUGHTS FOR IMPROVING THE NEXT SMOKE)
....
....
....
....
....

94

DATE ....

TITLE ....

MEAT ....
....

NOTES ....
....

WEIGHT ....

WOOD ....

PREPARATION
....

MARINADE/RUB

....

TIME	SMOKER/MEAT TARGET TEMP.	SMOKER ACTUAL TEMP.	MEAT TEMP.	SMOKER ADJUSTMENT MADE: ADDED COAL, WOOD CHIPS CHUNKS, MOPS, SAUCES, WRAPPED ETC..

TIME	SMOKER/MEAT TARGET TEMP.	SMOKER ACTUAL TEMP.	MEAT TEMP.	SMOKER ADJUSTMENT MADE: ADDED COAL, WOOD CHIPS CHUNKS, MOPS, SAUCES, WRAPPED ETC..

WEATHER
....

COOKING NOTES
....
....
....

RESULTS (AROMA, BARK, FLAVOR, TENDERNESS, MOISTURE, SMOKINESS)
....
....
....
....

RATING   1   2   3   4   5   6   7   8   9   10

ADDITIONAL NOTES (CHANGES, MODIFICATION, THOUGHTS FOR IMPROVING THE NEXT SMOKE)
....
....
....
....
....

DATE ....

TITLE ....

MEAT ....

NOTES ....

....

WEIGHT ....

WOOD ....

PREPARATION ....

MARINADE/RUB ....

....

TIME	SMOKER/MEAT TARGET TEMP.	SMOKER ACTUAL TEMP.	MEAT TEMP.	SMOKER ADJUSTMENT MADE: ADDED COAL, WOOD CHIPS CHUNKS, MOPS, SAUCES, WRAPPED ETC..

TIME	SMOKER/MEAT TARGET TEMP.	SMOKER ACTUAL TEMP.	MEAT TEMP.	SMOKER ADJUSTMENT MADE: ADDED COAL, WOOD CHIPS CHUNKS, MOPS, SAUCES, WRAPPED ETC..

WEATHER
....

COOKING NOTES
....
....
....

RESULTS (AROMA, BARK, FLAVOR, TENDERNESS, MOISTURE, SMOKINESS)
....
....
....

RATING   1   2   3   4   5   6   7   8   9   10

ADDITIONAL NOTES (CHANGES, MODIFICATION, THOUGHTS FOR IMPROVING THE NEXT SMOKE)
....
....
....
....
....

DATE ....

TITLE ....

MEAT ....
....

NOTES ....
....

WEIGHT ....

WOOD ....

PREPARATION ....
....

MARINADE/RUB ....
....

TIME	SMOKER/MEAT TARGET TEMP.	SMOKER ACTUAL TEMP.	MEAT TEMP.	SMOKER ADJUSTMENT MADE: ADDED COAL, WOOD CHIPS CHUNKS, MOPS, SAUCES, WRAPPED ETC..

TIME	SMOKER/MEAT TARGET TEMP.	SMOKER ACTUAL TEMP.	MEAT TEMP.	SMOKER ADJUSTMENT MADE: ADDED COAL, WOOD CHIPS CHUNKS, MOPS, SAUCES, WRAPPED ETC..

WEATHER
....

COOKING NOTES
....
....
....

RESULTS (AROMA, BARK, FLAVOR, TENDERNESS, MOISTURE, SMOKINESS)
....
....
....

RATING   1   2   3   4   5   6   7   8   9   10

ADDITIONAL NOTES (CHANGES, MODIFICATION, THOUGHTS FOR IMPROVING THE NEXT SMOKE)
....
....
....
....
....

DATE ....

TITLE
....

MEAT
....

NOTES
....

....

WEIGHT
....

WOOD

PREPARATION
....

....

MARINADE/RUB
....

....

TIME	SMOKER/MEAT TARGET TEMP.	SMOKER ACTUAL TEMP.	MEAT TEMP.	SMOKER ADJUSTMENT MADE: ADDED COAL, WOOD CHIPS CHUNKS, MOPS, SAUCES, WRAPPED ETC..

101

TIME	SMOKER/MEAT TARGET TEMP.	SMOKER ACTUAL TEMP.	MEAT TEMP.	SMOKER ADJUSTMENT MADE: ADDED COAL, WOOD CHIPS CHUNKS, MOPS, SAUCES, WRAPPED ETC..

WEATHER

COOKING NOTES

RESULTS (AROMA, BARK, FLAVOR, TENDERNESS, MOISTURE, SMOKINESS)

RATING   1   2   3   4   5   6   7   8   9   10

ADDITIONAL NOTES (CHANGES, MODIFICATION, THOUGHTS FOR IMPROVING THE NEXT SMOKE)

Made in United States
Troutdale, OR
12/11/2023